# Profit is the Byproduct of Efficiency: Conquering the Fear

*By*

*Jim Pierce*

The information printed herein represents the view of the author as of the date of the publication. This book is presented for information purposes only. The views expressed are those of the author alone, and should not be taken as expert instruction or commands. The reader is responsible for his or her own actions. While every attempt has been made to verify the information in this book, the author does not assume responsibility for errors, inaccuracies, or omissions.

Contact information. www.envoyofefficiency.info

ISBN 978-15309355574

Cover and Book designed by Jim Pierce

Edited by Madcat Information Services Corporation

Printed by CreateSpace, an Amazon.com Company

## Acknowledgements

This book is dedicated in memory of Roger C Clayton (1933-2011). A good friend who helped to mold me into the person I am today. He reminded me that my integrity is the legacy I shall leave upon this Earth.

Nothing can be accomplished in this world without the support of caring friends and family. This book is no exception. I would like to express a great deal of thanks to everyone who has helped me directly in the creation of this book.

A special thanks to the Resume Coach Debra Mastic http://www.debramastic.com/ for pushing me to get this book written. Also to Mary Self and Barbara Crosson for serving as victims, aka test readers. If these three ladies would have edited my book any more, I would have had to place them as co-authors.

I would also like to thank:
Fred Cornell, for his long-time friendship and advice.
Dale Callahan http://www.dalecallahan.com/, and
Anthony Witt http://tcepodcast.com/

All of these people kept reminding me that my long lost passion was in teaching and training others to be their best.

### *A Special Dedication to:*

I would like to issue a special dedication to the men and women in the University of Alabama at Birmingham's Information Engineering & Management Master Degree Program. My fellow classmates have served as a sounding board to my philosophies and ideas. In addition, the staff members have allowed me to refocus on my past experience and use it as a guiding light for decades to come.

INFORMATION ENGINEERING & MANAGEMENT

For more information about the IEM program at UAB go to http://www.uab.edu/engineering/iem/ or scan the QR code below.

# Table of Contents

*Profit is the Byproduct of Efficiency: Conquering the Fear*..........1

***Acknowledgements to***......................................................3

***A Special Dedication to:***....................................................4

*CONQUERING THE FEAR OF EFFICIENCY* ...........................10

APPREHENSION TO IMPROVEMENTS.....................14

WHY DO SOME IMPROVEMENTS FAIL?.................17

PLAGUED BY "IT WILL DO" .....................................19

SURROUNDED BY PARADOXES...............................21

MYTHS ABOUT EFFICIENCY.....................................23

SYSTEM EXPERTS HAVE FAILED THE SYSTEM ...25

SYSTEM DEVELOPMENT PROCESS........................27

CONSTRUCTING THE INVESTIGATION:.................28

Potential Stumbling Blocks ...............................................31

*PHASE 2: REQUIREMENTS* ....................................44

*PHASE 3: DEVELOPMENT* ......................................51

*PHASE 4: IMPLEMENTATION*.................................52

APPLIED EFFICIENCY...........................................................53

PLANNING A CRUISE (Create Savings) ......................56

Controlling Expenses..................................................57

Email Control (Workflow Efficiency)...........................61

Smart Purchasing (Purchasing Control) .......................65

Excessive UtilityBills: (Efficiency measures) .................70

Reducing Debt ...........................................................75

Cooking (Queueing theory) ........................................78

Not enough Toilet Paper (inventory control)..................83

5

HOME EFFICIENCY PROJECTS ...................................................88

    SECTION A. – SAVE MONEY ON UTILITIES ...........89

    SECTION B: COOKING ...............................................102

# A True Story

## (With only a few embellishments)

It was a crisp October afternoon, and Bob, a professor specializing in Operations Research and Mathematics, crossed the quad, the leaves from the maple trees crunching under his feet. The easterly wind, hinting at the winter to come, swooped in between the brick buildings which enclosed the square park. With a shiver, Bob turned up the collar of his sport coat and headed for the coffee shop at the corner of Smith Street and Lakeland Avenue.

Jim, a self-taught business consultant was already there, sitting at his usual table. Bob ordered a tall coffee with cream and joined him. After a while, the topic of conversation turned back to the one Bob brought up during their last meeting.

"I just can't understand it." Bob shrugged his shoulders in frustration. "You would think they wanted to lose money instead of make it."

For years Bob had been working with hospitals and universities to improve their internal processes and increase cash flow. He had met with success after success and was greeted almost as visiting royalty at each institution he visited. Yet there was one sector, where profits and increased cash flow are elevated to god-like status, which continued to turn him away. Corporation after corporation had closed their doors in Bob's face whenever he approached them with suggestions on how to improve their business.

"And it isn't just me," Bob continued. "I know of three other colleagues, one in Pittsburgh and the other two out west, who have received the same response. We know what we are doing, but businesses just don't want to listen."

He leaned forward, lowering his voice. "And you know what really gets me. I've discovered that later on some of these same businesses have adopted the very ideas I proposed to them. These guys read about them being used successfully in a research project I've done, and it's then that they decide to give my ideas a shot. Meanwhile, they've been losing money hand over fist. I just don't understand."

Jim savored the last swallow of coffee, and a mischievous smile grew as he set the cup down. "You know what the problem is? You don't speak with a MBA dialect."

Bob sat back, stunned, as Jim got to his feet. "Think about it," Jim said. "I'm going to get another cup. I'll be right back."

While he was gone, Bob's memory furiously replayed the various fruitless meetings he had with business executives and one face, its expression dulled by confusion, reappeared time and time again. By the time Jim returned, Bob understood. "Too much math?"

Jim smiled and nodded. "Too much math. See, most people make decisions based upon what they can conceive – our day-to-day reality. What people cannot understand, they fear. Business owners are no different. They can understand the physical reality of basic accounting – profit and loss, but once you move into the theoretical, you leave them and the average person behind. You have to keep it real."

# CONQUERING THE FEAR OF EFFICIENCY

It can be said that business efficiency begins at home. The business owner must be "hands on" with any type of efficiency improvement strategy. No matter how many consultants you bring into your company, you will always know more about your industry than the consultants. The fact that a business owner should take an active part in efficiency improvements has led some business owners to avoid the endeavor.

There are many reasons that a business owner may decide to avoid efficiency improvements. Some people feel they lack the time and/or resources needed to make their business more efficient. In some cases, fear is the number one obstacle. The fear is due to human anxiety caused by a lack of understanding of the problems. This is the obstacle that we will be looking at overcoming.

## THE HISTORY OF THIS GUIDE

Several years ago, the author began working on a project to develop a training program. The training program was designed to help small business owners to identify efficiency problems within their organizations. The process was supposed to be simple. All the author had to do was show the owners what to look for to identify efficiency problems and how to measure their findings. Indeed, this project was to be the pinnacle of the Envoy of Efficiency series.

When the author announced his plans to some of his colleagues, there was a lot of rejoicing. For the first time in history, business owners could be trained to help themselves. There were several business owners who were excited about the concept of a training program and could not wait to see a preview of it. The business owners' enthusiasm diminished rather quickly once they realized mathematics was involved. The game was over before the players took the field.

Just as the author had begun to abandon the project, he thought of an idea to reinvigorate the business owners. Since business efficiency starts at home, that is where the training should begin. Business owners could be trained to identify business efficiency problems if a training module was created to focus on efficiency in day-to-day life. The logic behind this is no one likes to fail or give the appearance of ignorance. This is especially true for small business owners and entrepreneurs. If you are in the privacy of your own home, no one can see you fail.

## WHO THIS GUIDE IS FOR

This guide has been designed for business owners as a method for building up their skills of investigation, observation and comparison. Even though the author has focused this guide on business owners, the efficiency knowledge it contains is in reference to day-to-day life and can be used by anyone. There are no specialized software packages or advanced calculations to remember. All topics covered in this guide can be found in a modern home or apartment.

## SPECIAL CONSIDERATIONS

This guide is also being released as a means of generating donations for two causes the author supports: The first of these causes is Veterans Empowerment Organizations. These are organizations who are dedicated to improving the quality of life for soldiers returning to civilian life and any veteran who wishes to better himself. Our focus will be on organizations with training programs designed to get soldiers back into the real world. The receiving organizations could be corporate training or a scholarship for colleges and universities.

The second cause the author champions is Animal Welfare. More specific, the author holds great reverence for animal shelters with a non-destroy policy. While these organizations do all they can to adopt out animals, keeping animals sheltered, vaccinated and fed requires donations. The receivers of these donations could be animal welfare organizations of all types or a humble homeowner who takes care of the feeding, sheltering and medical needs of incoming strays.

## Downloading supporting files

**All users:** All supporting files from this book can be found in the download section of the Envoy of Efficiency website. The items will be identified by book/chapter and should be easy to locate. The author reserves the right to add new files to the support area to better assist the reader at understanding the principles of the book. The URL has been provided below. If any other files would be helpful, feel free to contact the author.

**Kindle users:** Since many photos, charts and illustrations cannot be easily viewed from a Kindle or other online media library, you will need to download them from the Envoy of Efficiency website from a laptop or computer in order to gain the most benefit from the book.

Website URL: http://www.envoyofefficiency.info/downloads

Process Improvement? It really chills me to the bone!

APPREHENSION TO IMPROVEMENTS

People have a tendency to believe what they can see, conceive or visualize. Unlike a building, a process takes no true physical form. Therefore, the system owner has no way to assign a dollar value cost to each piece of structural material used in creating it. Nor can they see a return on investment for each piece of occupied office space. If there is a lack of visualization, fear creeps into the mind of the business owner. This is the **fear of no control**.

A second reason people are apprehensive about launching efficiency improvements is the **fear of misunderstanding**. This fear is created because the business owner may not know exactly where to start or stop the modifications. No one wants to make a trip down an unfamiliar road without a map to guide them. Compounding the fear is the lack of a well-defined destination.

This fear is due to a lack of understanding fundamental concepts of industrial engineering. Let us make no mistakes: efficiency is about manipulating a process within a system. Systems analysis is a key fundamental to understanding where to only begin and end with modifications. The people who have been exposed to some level of learning of system efficiency have received incomplete pieces of knowledge which would have come in an extremely painful setting.

The third primary reason people are apprehensive to launch efficiency improvements are due to the **fear of failure**. In his book *Tribes*(Godin), Seth Godin pointed out the concepts of how people are connected with leaders and ideas. The ideas the leader has delivered unto his tribe are supposed to remain strong. Nothing which could weaken the idea should *ever* be done.

Frightened by the possibility of potential failure in front of their employees, business owners stay clear of change. Business owners are less likely to buy into a project they feel would diminish the respect their employees have for them. This variable is hard for small business owners to overcome regardless of the rewards which await them.

The benefits and rewards for efficiency can only be realized once the business owner puts forth the effort to understand the realm of efficiency as it relates to process improvement. While this may seem an easy task, process improvement usually generates an uneasy feeling. Process improvement is related to industrial engineering. Applying industrial engineering principles without being an industrial engineer usually translates into certain failure in the mind of business owners.

## I can figure it out, I'm an Ivy League Graduate

# WHY DO SOME IMPROVEMENTS FAIL?

Failures are a key part of business. In 1990, Dan Miller coined "Icarus Paradox" (Miller) in his book with the same title. The term is used to identify business failures caused by the element which has previously given it success. In many respects, Icarus Paradox is the best way to describe a process improvement within a system.

Process improvement is a paradox in its truest form. The system in which a process is parented is itself a paradox which creates problems by its very existence. In some cases, a company can spend more time and money maintaining a new process than it would have spent using an old inefficient one. Does this mean the process is flawed? Not in the least. It sometimes means the metrics used need to be expanded to include elements outside of the process.

If you launch a helium filled balloon into the sky you never truly know which compass direction it will travel unless you have up to the minute atmospheric data. You only know that it will travel up. Or do you? Barometric pressure could burst the balloon before you let it go. Case and point, you have to pay close attention to the measurements you have under control and even closer attention to the ones you do not have under control.

In brief, process improvement at its core can be best identified as a problem remediation. People are dealing with problems every day. At every moment of every day there are people dealing with process problems throughout the world. War exists because the peace processes of the world are broken. The planet Earth is a type of system. Each nation on Earth is a smaller system. Within each nation, a series of processes are all working at the same time. These processes are all looking for a finite amount of resources within a system. When the systems run out of resources, they look to other systems for them. Does this remind you of anything? Does it remind you why wars are started?

One may ask why problem remediation is important within a system. The best answer is because most systems are flawed at the time of their creation. Many of them work poorly, if they work at all. This problem is compounded once you have multiple systems operating in close proximity to one another. Systems do not always play well with each other. Even though systems don't always work well together, the designer will usually become complacent and think things will work out just fine.

The worst thing that can happen is approaching a process improvement with a sense of complacency. Complacency may leave the designer with the sense of accomplishment, but it may also create flaws which are worse than the unmodified process. There are only two proper outcomes for a designed process improvement. The process improvement either meets criteria or it does not meet criteria. There is not a third outcome for process improvement to suggest "it will do".

Tired of tweaking the work-flow, it is inevitable for some business owners to look at the final product and feel that it is close enough to his vision. This is to be expected of anyone who designs the initial system of a business. However, the system is only going to work the way you want it to work if you can answer the following questions honestly and accurately.

WHAT DO I NEED?

DOES THIS ACCOMPLISH WHAT I NEED IT TO?

DOES THIS FULFILL MY VISION?

WHAT IS THE COST OF THE BETTER MODEL?

WHAT ARE THE BENEFITS OF THE BETTER MODEL?

Regardless of how many problems are being overcome in a process, always try to eliminate them all in a single integration. The outcomes of your process efficiency improvement should meet all criteria a designer has established for it. There is nothing more damning than partially correcting a problem. A partially corrected problem will lead to a complacent final product. The outcome of the new process will be less than stellar if it works at all.

It is difficult at times for some people to remember that the processes they create for their business are actually for their customers' benefit. If you are advertising a ten out of ten customer experience rating, do not try to give the customer a five out of ten experience; they know the difference. Customers will realize something is not right even if the process is in a back office which will never be seen. The customer knows what to expect because you are advertising it. Even if it is not advertised, the customer will still realize that your process is flawed.

Do you need an example? Try to imagine a salesman at Harley Davidson motorcycles trying to sell a professional biker a scooter with the HD logos on it. A professional biker will not be content with the scooter. It is not what the biker envisioned; nor will it be the sales experience he expected. The biker may say a few three word phrases to the salesman, but "it will do" is not going to be among the phrases.

With the looming sense of dread, you are probably imagining the outcome of that poor salesman. His fate is not to be your problem. Your problem shall be to train your mind to first identify a system. Once you see the system, you will then be able to see the paradoxes within them. So, where do you go when you want to look for a system? No need to look too hard, they are closer than you may think.

Systems, whether efficient or inefficient, are around us at any time of the day. We have become a society reliant on systems. Correction: we have become a society created by systems. The concept of a 9 to 5 work day is itself a conventional process embedded by grade schools to support a system of norms within the American society. The most successful entrepreneurs have learned to reject such predefined processes and create their own processes thus redefining the system to fulfill their needs.

In this day and age, no one can afford to not have a basic understanding of how to correct inefficiencies found within a systems. It was mentioned earlier that a system's very existence creates a paradox. Some of the paradoxes created must be remedied in order to allow a system to achieve its true potential. The only way to have true understanding is to educate people about how their system works and how paradoxes occur within their system.

Conventional wisdom states that systems must be modified by an industrial engineer. Nowhere is it chiseled in stone that only the industrial engineer should understand how the system functions. This is especially true for a system owned by a company. While it is not unusual for an industrial engineer to work for a company, they rarely hold a C-level position while working as an industrial engineer. Why do industrial engineers usually not hold C-level positions?

Industrial engineers are trained to be the best at structure, redundancy, and formation of a system to service a company. While it is not uncommon to see industrial engineers focus on a single industry, it is rare to see them become intimate at a company level. This is because industrial engineers usually have their pulse on industry trends. If they were to become too focused with company administration, they may lose sight of new improvements within the industry.

In a nutshell, the most focused person on business process efficiency must remain focused on the outside of the business. On the other hand, the person who owns and understands the most intimate details within a business, doesn't understand the systems which make it so successful. Does anyone else see the irony with this logic? Congratulations, you have just found your first paradox. Now is the time for this paradox to be corrected.

As luck would have it, this entire book has been written to remedy this paradox. This is the first step to give the business system back to the business owner. Before you get too excited and decide to dive right into the lesson, we need to first take a look at eliminating the fear of understanding. This can best be accomplished by dispelling the myths associated with process improvement and system efficiency.

# MYTHS ABOUT EFFICIENCY

## Efficiency Improvements are Expensive

It is a common belief that improving the efficiency of a company is an expensive endeavor. Nothing could be farther from the truth. As a matter of fact, many actions for small businesses to improve efficiency involve very little costs. Furthermore, there are many actions which require no money at all.

This book will be outlining ways to improve efficiency that require very little money. While the methods used in this book will require very little money and no technical knowledge, they do require a keen sense of observation and logic. The fact that this book's exercises are to be implemented inside one's own home should have no impact on the amount of observation which should be used. The better a person becomes at identifying problems inside the home will reinforce a good habit which will follow them into the business environment.

## Efficiency is about Increasing Profits

Efficiency is about process improvement and has nothing to do with profits or money. This is why the program has been titled "Profit is the Byproduct of Efficiency". For decades, efficiency experts have used profits as a measuring stick to sell their products. This is nothing more than a psychological ploy to get you to buy the product and put your company's fate in their hands.

True efficiency consultants use an industrial engineering approach to uncovering inefficiencies within processes. They use structured methodologies to uncover process problems and quantifiable measurements to discover hidden opportunities of improvement. It is this concept of process improvement that eliminates waste and reduces costs.

When revenues remain the same and costs decrease, profits naturally increase.

### Efficiency must be 100% or it is worthless.

Efficiency is not an all or nothing endeavor. In some processes achieving 100% efficiency is catastrophic over time. In the author's opinion, a well-designed system should perform between 85% to 95% efficiency at any given time. It is best to think of efficiency like a rubber band; it cannot be stretched to its full potential for very long or it will surely break.

While it may seem counter-intuitive for an efficiency consultant (who nags people to be more efficient day, after day, after day) to advise people to not shoot for 100% efficiency, it is best for the system as a whole. After all, a sprinter cannot run at top speed for the duration of a marathon: nor can a company's machines or employees. The only measurable outcome for processes functioning at 100% is the decrease in time before the system fails. Just for clarification, operating at 100% efficiency is not efficient.

The establishment of standards for efficient operations depends entirely on what a system is being used to accomplish. A computer controlled process should function closer to the 95% mark, with the remaining 5% used as maintenance. Whereas a process involving human interaction on an assembly line should function at only 85%, with the remaining 15% used to maintain the system. The only way to understand how efficient a system should be requires looking through libraries of information.

## SYSTEM EXPERTS HAVE FAILED THE SYSTEM

Within the vast libraries throughout the world, there exists tens of thousands of books, articles, and scientific papers precisely documenting the efficiency of systems and what makes them inefficient. These tomes of wisdom make themselves available only to the most knowledgeable of men. They are hidden away as if they were in vaults of sorcery availing themselves only to the wizards of a secret society. It is the making of a great fiction book, "Harry Potter and the Secret Vaults of Efficiency". I'm not sure if J. K. Rowling will be drafting this one any time soon. Probably not.

Getting back to reality; if one were to scour through the vast libraries they would have a difficult time locating a basic primer of systems or efficiency improvement.   The vast majority of these publications are written in a strange, almost forgotten, language known as mathematics. Where are the basic guides designed for mortals? They do not exist. For this reason, the system experts have failed the system.

As was mentioned in earlier writings in the case of Bob, business leaders need a way to comprehend what is being discussed with them. The hospitals and universities in which Bob collaborates are full of people who are fluent in the language of mathematics. These organizations house those individuals who have access to the great vaults of sorcery yet lack the time to immerse themselves within the myriad tomes.

Let us suppose that while exploring the universe we were to discover a stone-age race of humans living on Mars. If we were to demonstrate to them how to make a fire with a lighter, we would witness excitement among them as it would be an easier way to make fire. On the other hand, if we were to start using the fire to heat up ore to make steel, they might get the wrong idea about what our diet consists of. "Why in the heck are they cooking rocks for dinner? We have venison!"

While this may seem to be a far-fetched example, in reality it is more accurate than one would think. Industrial engineers try to promote their benefits to owners of companies while using engineering language. If company owners spoke the engineering language, they would probably be engineers. Instead, most business owners speak with an MBA dialect. They understand some of the mathematics associated with engineering, but don't expect them to deliver a lecture on the topic.

How much do you understand about system efficiency? For most people throughout the world, this answer will be very little. The only way for a business owner to truly understand is to put their boots on the ground and walk a few steps into the world of industrial engineering. This is the best and only real way to gain a better understanding. So let's take that first baby step and develop our own system.

# DEVELOPING THE EFFICIENT SYSTEM
## SYSTEM DEVELOPMENT PROCESS

Discovering ways to improve process efficiency requires significant effort. In order to determine what needs to be fixed, one must first identify the existing structure. For this to occur, one needs a general understanding about how a particular system works. These concepts will allow a better understanding of efficiency and will move you to the next level of efficiency analysis. The remainder of this section deals with the actual process of crafting the research and the author, unfortunately, must remain a little more serious than usual.

As the business owner, you know better than any consultant what you want to do and how your processes interact with one another. You can pick up on problems that a professional researcher may overlook because you know your own field better than any professional. In addition, you will hear about new ideas and be referred to newer technologies that an expert may have never encountered.

You may not believe this statement, but before you dispel it, here is something to think about. The more levels of personnel between yourself and a specific job in your organization, the less likely you are to know about individual problems your staff encounters on the job. Furthermore, if you are this far removed from a job within your own industry and company, imagine how far removed a professional researcher would be. The author only claims to be an expert in the field of operations research and process improvement. Unless your company resides in one of these two fields, the author would consider you more of an industry expert than he is.

How long will it take you to conduct the analysis of your processes? Not as long as you might think. You probably already know, or think you know, where improvements can be made. Your analysis becomes even easier if you have already constructed a process flowchart. If you have not already constructed a process flowchart, do not worry. You will be shown how to properly construct one later in this book. For now, your primary task is to get yourself into the proper mindset.

You may believe that hiring professional analysts is the way to go at this point in time. However, the more complex your organization is and the more processes your organization possesses, the more expensive the project will be. In addition, the experience of 'doing it yourself' will give you unique insight into your organization which will allow you to understand its full growth potential and limitations. Moreover, this experience remains with you even if you were to leave your organization. It takes you one step closer to becoming a true expert in your field, if not a leading authoritative figure.

CONSTRUCTING THE INVESTIGATION:

All efficiency improvements require a certain level of research to be done prior to implementing. Careful attention must be placed on the processes to be changed. Attention should also be focused on other processes which rely on the processes that are being changed. It is for these reasons that a research plan and report should be constructed for every efficiency improvement regardless how insignificant it may seem.

A standard report regardless of type can be requested in three ways. First, a person may ask for the information to be compiled for them.

Second, the report could be generated as part of an organization's standard operating procedures. Third, an individual may compile the report on their own initiative. The way a report is generated can determine what information may have been missed. Understanding how a report was developed will be very useful when you begin to define the problem as it can help uncover hidden truths.

It makes no sense to build a report if you do not know exactly what it is being built for. It is easy enough to say that a report is being built to provide information. The difference presents itself when you ask yourself the reason the report is providing information. For instance, you build an automobile to satisfy the need for transportation, but are there additional needs? Of course there are other needs to be considered.

If general transportation was the only reason to build an automobile, we would all still be driving Model T Fords. But what about speed? Cargo room? Passenger comfort? Each automobile owner has their own requirements, and likewise, in order to properly construct a report one must understand the exact need to be satisfied.

One type of report satisfies the need for information. These types of reports are usually filled with data and usually include a quantitative type of representation of the data. These reports are usually a representation of current data as it exists in the present. These types of reports are produced to provide others with information. In some cases, these reports are used as a basis of comparison for research studies. A country's official economic outlook report is one such report.

The second type of report outlines a specific problem to be solved. These reports are usually generated as an inquiry to understand cause and effect information. In business applications, these reports usually define options for future activities. They represent what things could be like if certain actions are (or are not) taken. These are the types of reports we will be primarily be focusing on for efficiency analysis.

# Potential Stumbling Blocks

*Clarity of the problem*

A great injustice to efficiency is the lack of understanding of the real problem. It is not uncommon for a business owner to say their problem is that a process is not producing enough work to keep up with demand. Knowing this, an efficiency expert will quickly start to dissect the process and find ways to improve each step. This is the normal response and a solution is soon to be discovered. But was this really the problem?

The author takes pride in his unorthodox approach to efficiency. He understands that a process is an inanimate being and cannot have a problem. While others follow the standard procedure and begin analyzing the process, the author begins by questioning the client further.

It all boils down to the answering the real question: what does the client really want? What is their pain? What is the real problem they have with the way things are now? Is this problem even within the realm of a process engineer to correct? These questions may seem odd for a consultant to be asking but let us take a close look at the implications these questions could reveal.

In the previous scenario the client stated the process was not producing enough work to keep up with demand. In several situations, the author discovered the clients were afraid of losing money due to unfulfilled sales. This was their pain!  Using this information, the author soon discovered the client's products were being sold at an extreme discount compared to the competition. Increasing the client's prices actually corrected the balance of supply and demand while still affording the client a modest increase in profits. This move was more profitable to the client than reengineering the system to increase the supply.

Every problem has a need to be fulfilled. One careful consideration that should never be taken lightly is that the need for efficiency research is ultimately about people. It is easy for a business owner to say one thing but in fact the problem stems from a deeper need. These needs are usually not directly associated with what the owners perceive to be their pain. In order to truly uncover the real pain, you must follow these two rules.

The first rule is that if the problem was given to you orally, ask more questions and take notes. In order to be an effective efficiency consultant, one must also be a counselor with a sympathetic ear. The more people talk about their problem, the more likely an underlying problem will reveal itself. Marketing experts have proven that everyone has an image in their mind which they associate with their personal happiness. You must try to get your clients to share that image with you. This applies to spouse, employees, or actual customers. Everyone has a bigger picture.

The second rule is, if the problem is written out, look for points for analysis. Pay less attention to what is written down and look for what is missing from the document. A good analogy; people contact the police to report the car being stolen. After listening to the claimant's story one of the first questions the responding officer asks is whether the keys were in the car. This one piece of information is usually omitted from the car owner's story. In brief, look at what is written down, and then look for what information is not readily available.

If you deal with research of any type, you will eventually run into incomplete information. Efficiency research endeavors are no different. There will always be more information needed than what is provided. This is especially true if the business owner has not completely identified the real motive for the outcome to be addressed. Surprising as it may seem, this problem occurs more often than people are led to believe.

It is the author's opinion that a new research study should always be conducted with a blank slate. Take all information provided, dissect it, and rebuild it. These actions, while sometimes redundant, can uncover more information than by simply accepting information provided to the researcher. This will also eliminate biased information which may have been presented as accurate data. There are two ways to deal with incomplete information.

The first way is for the researcher to make logical interpretations of the information being presented. This method requires the researcher to have industry experience and direct knowledge about industry standards.  It is not uncommon to find specialized industry consultants who, at one point in time, worked within the particular industry for which they now consult.  This is also a good reason for business owners to take it upon themselves to learn to be a researcher. No one knows an industry better than someone who currently works within the industry.

The second way is for the researcher to gain information from literary resources. For decades, the largest problem with assimilating information for research has been determining where to look for such information. The internet, search engines specifically, has streamlined the process of trying to locate relevant information. The task of identifying data sources which used to take weeks and lots of driving can now be accomplished in an afternoon in front of a computer. Indeed, the problem of locating relevant data has now been changed to the problem of having to weed out less relevant data.

Between to two scenarios, having too much information is always better than having too little. A researcher can always cluster commonalities with too much information. However, it is hard to get the complete picture when information is scarce.

*Proprietary Information:*

For creating a report which relies heavily on proprietary data, you should go directly to the source of the information and look at the raw data available. Sometimes when dealing with proprietary data the sources are not readily available for the researcher to review. In these circumstances, the researcher should take special precautions to identify the information in the report as assumptions.

Furthermore, do not be surprised if the proprietary data provided becomes a problem later in the investigation. There are cases where people who control the data wish to improve the image of the data and the contribution it makes to the company. The author has seen cases where the proprietary data was merged with another data set in order to improve the outcome totals. As was previously mentioned, if you are relying on proprietary data without access to review the source, report it as an assumption.

*Identifying Assumptions:*

Whenever a researcher includes information outside of his control, an assumption has just been located. Assumptions should be defined precisely on a report as it could change the outcome if these variables change. By identifying assumptions in a report, you are saying that if the assumption is true, you can guarantee the outcome. It is not good enough to simply state the assumption you are making. You need to justify that each assumption is probably true or the research should not continue.

For instance, if you are conducting a feasibility study on the efficiency of using solar energy for electricity in a building, you can and should make the following assumptions: (a) the sun will reach the solar panels for an average amount of time; (b) solar panels and all associated components will be for sale on the market; and (c) average energy consumption will remain constant and will not dramatically increase.

None of these things can be guaranteed, but you must justify your assumptions by including supportive data. Such as; (a) the average amount of sunlight per year for the past ten or twenty years has been ## days; (b) the components for solar power has been readily available for ## years and more are being manufactured; (c) and average energy consumption for the building has been ## units and should continue to be near that amount.

### Identifying limitations

Limitations in a research report or feasibility study are factors of imperfect information which are not in your control. Limitations are potential weaknesses and you must be able to try to compensate for them. A good example of a limitation is when you need sales data is for a certain product over a certain length of time, but the product has just been released. Instead, you use sales data for a comparable product on the market and identify any differences between the products which could negate the data.

*Initial investigation:*

Managers, regardless of whether they are a company CEO or the Head of a household, need a way to evaluate ideas without committing a lot of resources. The initial investigation phase allows this to happen. The initial investigation provides enough of a general analysis to determine whether a request warrants further study. This is the end of some projects and the beginning for others.

When properly used, the initial investigation can save a great deal of time and effort. A properly prepared initial investigation will allow a steering committee to make a decision to terminate a request at this point. Upon termination, especially in the case of incomplete information, the steering committee can elect to provide feedback to the investigator as to what further information should be included or clarified prior to the investigation being resubmitted.

*Feasibility Study:*

In the event further study is recommended, the initial investigation passes on to step two of the planning phase – the feasibility study. There are many interpretations of what a feasibility study is and why it is created. For the purposes of this book, a feasibility study is a method of identifying risks associated with process improvements which could cause a system to fail prior to deployment.

The feasibility study is broken into several components. These components will be looked at on the next page. Each of these components serves to look at specific pieces of information required to make an educated decision.

The overall function of the feasibility study is to provide the steering committee with enough information about a project to determine if it should be launched. A feasibility study can be as formal or informal as the creator chooses to make it.

*Common Feasibility Study Outline*

I.     Executive summary

II.    Introduction

    a.  Purpose

    b.  Audience

III.   Justification

    a.  Problem statement

    b.  Organizational Impact

    c.  Business Impact

    d.  Process impact

    e.  Solution Objectives

IV.    Solution

    a.  Solution Statement

    b.  Anticipated Improvements

    c.  Impact

    d.  Rationale

V.     Alternatives

    a.  Alternatives Description

    b.  Comparison Matrix

VI.    Cost-Benefit Analysis

    a.  Approach and Tools

    b.  Values

A prefabricated feasibility study template can be downloaded from the Envoy of Efficiency website.

Now that you have seen the large scale outline of the common feasibility study, we are going to take a step in a different direction. Forget about the outline! It is the opinion of the author that a feasibility study is one of the most overused, cumbersome, and inefficient documents in the business world. There is very little need for a formal feasibility study in the new world economy.

The feasibility study is a true masterpiece of information created by sadists. It was possibly developed to allow company executives to put off crucial decisions by saying a study is needed first. Perhaps it is to keep executives so busy they cannot see their staff goofing off. "Do you need three more days off, we will alter all the calculations, call it Revision One and slide it under the CEO's door. See you in Tijuana."

As mentioned before, the overall function of the feasibility study is to provide the steering committee with enough information about a project to determine if it should be launched. Regardless of the format or outline you use to conduct the feasibility study, you only need to answer the following questions.

Is there a demand/need for the process?

Who else is using this process?

What problems can we expect by switching to this process?

What are the resources required to make the process work?

What are the costs associated with producing the process?

Which costs are fixed and which are variable?

How much can we expect to save/gain by implementing this?

When you look at the feasibility study in this format, it is not as scary. The simplicity of the question and answer format delivers structure to the document while preserving the natural flow of language and thought.

Let us take a quick look at these questions in order to give you a better understanding of why these questions are important.

### Is there a demand/need for the process?

In order for any change to occur, there must be a demonstrated need for change. The objective of this question to determine whether this process is viable and if it will solve the need. This question should clarify why you are looking at using this process.

### Who else is using this process?

Whenever you look at adopting a process, it is best to learn about previous deployments with other organizations. This question creates a list of companies and people to go-to for more information.

### What problems can we expect by switching to this process?

This question links directly to the information provided in the previous question. Consulting previous users can provide you with vital information. Knowing what successes, and more importantly, what difficulties they encountered can help you implement your process more smoothly.

**What are the resources required to make the process work??**

Every process will require tangible resources in order to be created. This question helps to determine the people, places and things (aka nouns) needed to create the process. Be as specific as possible.

With respect to personnel, sometimes you may not know exactly what personnel are needed. In this circumstance, it can be better to create an avatar with the skill sets needed by the person in the position.

**What are the costs associated with producing the process?**

Welcome to the business world, everything has a price. A continuation of the previous question, this question is used to quantify the price of the nouns you will need to create the process.

**Which costs are fixed and which are variable?**

Now that you know how much money you need in your piggy bank, you now need to see the amount of variations in the costs structure for the end process. You also need to understand the amount of money needed to create the product created by the process. This question allows you to see which costs are fixed and which are variable.

Once this is done, you will able to quickly determine the breakeven point and efficiency level. This is done by adjusting the increments of unit production of the variable costs.

**How much can we expect to save/gain by implementing this process?**

Ladies and Gentlemen, this question helps you grasp the brass-ring. This is the payoff for all of your hard work and it allows you to justify the existence of the newly created process.

In today's world, it is not good enough to say "we can save a boat-load of money". You need to be able to quantify the amount of each type of savings. If this is not for true financial saving, you must still demonstrate your gains in a quantifiable way.

In today's average home:

"It will reduce time to wash a car by 15 minutes"

"Reduce energy bill by $100 per month"

"Decrease dinner prep time by 10 minutes"

This also translates to the business world:

"It will improve number of widgets created by 15%"

"Reduce personnel training costs by $2500 per month"

"Decrease customer service time by 80%"

## PHASE 2: REQUIREMENTS

*Operations and Systems Analysis:*

Logic states if you change a process within a system then you need to understand exactly what elements within the system will be changed. With this in mind, one must also understand what other elements outside of the process must also be changed to accommodate the new process.

The best known method for mapping out how a system will function is to create a process flowchart. A process flowchart is a visual representation of what happens at every stage of a process. The stages are linked together with arrows to demonstrate the flow of succession. Even the smallest change in a process can make a dramatic change in a system. We should take a closer look at this.

Let us suppose that we improve our workstations to automate certain functions for the human user. By doing this we reduce the workstation completion time from 10 to 4 minutes. While this seems to be a great achievement, we must also look at what it does for the next and parallel processes. If parallel processes still take 8-10 minutes to complete, then we have just created a bottleneck at the next process. These are the variables which must be accounted for when changing a process.

A process flowchart is sometimes confused with a workstation flowchart; a mapping of workstations within a process or system. A process flowchart is actually a more detailed than a work flowchart. A process flowchart can best be thought of as a method of micro-managed steps inside of a process.

44

For example: In a work station flow chart for an online book selling business may look like this:

1. Customer selects book to buy.
2. Customer places order.
3. Order is received at office.
4. Office notifies warehouse of order.
5. Warehouse ships book to customer.

If you were to try and optimize the online book ordering process using a workstation flowchart the task would be impossible.The workstation flowchart does not contain enough useable information for process optimization to occur. While this information is accurate and useable at the corporate level, it holds no merit for what we are trying to accomplish.

In order to create a successful improvement to process efficiency, more data must be made available. You need to be able to see step-by-step decisions and tasks. In order for you to better understand what is being discussed, you need to see the data used in a process flowchart.

A process flowchart will look like this:

1. Customer selects book to buy.
   a. Verify title is available. If Yes, then go to 2. Otherwise return to 1.
2. Customer places order

a. Check customer password. If good, go to b. Otherwise DISREGARD TRANSACTION. Allow customer to log in to account.

b. Verify payment amount, if good, go to c. Otherwise DISREGARD TRANSACTION.

c. Verify payment type. If good, go to d. Otherwise DISREGARD TRANSACTION, allow customer to select new payment type and return to c.

d. Verify transaction approval. If good, ORDER HAS BEEN PLACED, go to 3. Otherwise DISREGARD TRANSACTION

3. Order is received at office.

a. Has payment has been received:

i. Yes. Go to 4.

ii. No. Hold order until (i) is satisfied or cancel transaction and reimburse customer.

4. Office notifies warehouse of order.

a. Associate pulls book from inventory and updates inventory count.

b. Book is sent to packaging.

5. Warehouse ships book to customer

# Symbols for a Flowchart

| Symbol | Represents | Example |
|---|---|---|
| ⬭ | Start/Stop | Receive complaint<br>Receive request<br>Proposal |
| ◇ | Decision Point | Yes/No<br>Agree/Disagree<br>Pass/Fail |
| ▭ | Activity | Hold a meeting<br>Make a phone call<br>Send a request |
| ⬓ | Document | Report is completed<br>Meeting minutes<br>Form is filled out |
| ○ | Connector | Go to another page or another part of the flowchart |
| ⌓ | Delay | Waiting for a service<br>Report sitting on a desk |

*Content copied from NC Department of Environment and Natural Resources*

*User requirements:*

Once you have determined the process flow, an investigator's next step is to find out what resources are needed by the user at each of these steps. The user requirements are the most overlooked component of the feasibility study. Many investigators assume they know what goes on and bypass the user. This leads to many problems within a process improvement. This is especially true whenever technology improvements are involved.

The reason why user requirements are so important when a technology improvement is involved is because some vendors do not update software on a routine basis. If the software used to perform a task is not designed to work on the newest operating systems, the new system will not work. There is nothing more frustrating for you or your staff than realizing you just spent a great deal of time and money for a product which will not work.

The user requirements area is where your employees tell you about their comfort level. This is also the area where the fear of failure can be controlled. Your understanding of the system will strengthen when employees give you more input about the process. Not only does this improve the potential process improvement, but it also improves morale. Employees want respect. Asking for their opinions and ideas gives you a better understanding of the process. This also gives employees a sense of belonging within the company. You are able to help them to help themselves while they are helping you.

Business owners worry about launching a bad efficiency improvement. Whenever you bring your team together to help you to improve the way work is done, you are minimizing the chance of failure. In the event that it does fail, no one is going to be pointing the finger at you. Your employees have become conspirators in the race for efficiency. Success is done as a team, failure should be no different.

*Support Appraisal:*

If people are to be using a new process to generate work, there should be a best known method in place for use with the new process. The Best Known Method, BKM for short, is the system/industrial engineer's (SIE) recommended way of performing an action. The BKM is generated by collecting and analyzing data.

A SIE will look at many variables when creating a BKM. While completion time (Increased Quantity) is the primary driver of most BKMs, it is not always considered the BKM. The reason why BKMs may be different from one company to the next is because each company will focus on one of three improvement goals governing production. The three primary goals for any process improvement are improved quantity, improved quality, and improved price. Once the BKM has been established the SIE will create BKM documentation.

Whenever dealing with a change in technology or other process improvements, it is wise to create training materials based on the SIE documentation. These materials can be in the form of a written manual, a video or both. Whatever the method, the training materials must be able to show the process from start to finish. A well designed training program will discuss why something is done in a certain way. This extra little touch will allow the user to understand the process even more. The training program also allows the user to identify problems which may not have been observed by the SIE at the time the BKM was created.

*Evaluating Alternatives:*

There are usually multiple ways to perform any task. A feasibility study will not only focus on the primary method, it will also look for alternative methods of accomplishing a task. Whenever an investigator lists and evaluates alternatives, he is actually giving himself a backup method of accomplishing tasks. These alternate methods come in handy when the primary method encounters barriers which cannot be readily overcome.

Any small change in the way the task is completed is considered to be an alternative. This could be something as small as removing an automatic stapler from a desk. It could also be as complex as building a new facility. Even the smallest change in a process can make a dramatic change in a system.

There is no way to sugar coat this next piece of information. A system is like a child. Once created, it stays with a company forever. It is now up to the parent, i.e. the company, to train the system to be the best it can be in order to make the parent proud. The parent can be hands-on and train the child to be an academic scholar who always delivers the best it can. Alternatively, the parent can be hands-off and allow the child to grow into a mischievous prankster who brings chaos into the work environment. The way you train your system is your choice.

This principle holds true for existing systems that need to be altered to make them more efficient. In this case, we can think of them more as adolescent systems. The systems are already present when a company and its current systems, are purchased, inherited or acquired in some other manner. In other words, a mature system automatically becomes an adolescent system when it changes ownership. A shift in corporate control is actually a shift in the corporate system. This is similar to the way a child behaves with his grandparents when his parents are not around.

*Changes to Come:*

It would be naïve to assume that change is easy. In reality, the greatest threat to any efficiency improvement endeavor is the neglect of monitoring changes occurring in the organization. Changing processes within an organization is like cooking soup on the stove; you must keep observing the mixture and stirring to distribute heat to all parts of the pot. There are no spoons or ladles in the business world but, there are milestones, measurements, and mathematics.

Like a soup, the process must be continually sampled to make certain the taste remains well-balanced and pleasing. Sometimes adjustments, perhaps a tad more pepper, need to be made; sometimes the process is fine just the way it is. The quality and availability of ingredients, or in the case of processes, resources can change. In this case, both you and the process must be flexible to accommodate the change. Inflexibility is a recipe for disaster.

## APPLIED EFFICIENCY

You have officially finished the most boring parts of this book. You now get to focus on the real reason why you bought this book. We are going to take scenarios, some comical in nature, and allow you to focus on becoming a lean, mean efficiency machine.

It is now time you begin applying information found in the previous sections to actual problems found throughout the home. Each one of these sections will contain a problem that is similar to a common business problem. Each one of these problems has been designed to make you think about the logical flow of process improvement. The corresponding business application of these problems has been included to allow for easier visualization.

While some of these examples may seem comical in nature, these are all real problems found in a majority of homes throughout the world. If the reader implements these within his own home, financial and/or time savings will occur. Even more savings will occur if a business owner deploys the business counterpart within his organization.

**Remember: Efficiency has nothing to do with money.**

Efficiency is about process improvement. Any part of a system that has rules which govern it in order to control outcomes can be considered a process. The *Profit is the Byproduct of Efficiency* Series is about creating efficiency through process improvement. Increased profit may or may not be a direct result of the improvements made.

A special chapter titled *Home Efficiency Projects* has been included at the end of this book to speed up the process of data review. The data are clustered into sections to make them easier to locate. This allows you to focus on specific areas of efficiency improvements. These improvements can be launched without a feasibility study, but it is best to create one in order to gain the full experience and wisdom of process improvement. By correctly applying the methods within these sections you can realize both monetary and time savings with minimal effort,

Applied learning in a controlled environment is the best way to teach anyone, specifically, business owners how to properly deploy process efficiency improvements. The following scenarios walk you through the processes you have been learning throughout this book. These include a step-by-step approach to demonstrate to you how easy it is to launch efficiency improvement efforts. In your home, there are no employees to criticize you if you get it wrong.

## First Exercise:

This exercise is designed to get you to thinking about how efficiency improvements can be used to free up resources. Simply follow the directions below:

On a sheet of paper, write down the amount of funds you have immediately available to spend on home efficiency improvement. Example: "I only have $**&lt;insert amount here&gt;**to be used on efficiency improvements". This is the estimated budget you have to launch efficiency improvements.

On the same sheet of paper, write down the monetary amount of savings you feel you need to perform a certain goal. Example: "I need to free up $**&lt;insert amount here&gt;**in order to **&lt;Insert goal here&gt;**".

Note: Be sure to include the task that you will be performing in the last space. For an individual, the task could be "to pay off credit cards", "build a garage", or "save up for vacation". The sky is the limit but make sure that you have a focus.

This information will be used to create the baseline on what dollar amount efficiency improvements may be needed. This actually creates your goal. More specific, you have identified the amount of how much savings you need to free up; you have identified your goal; and you have identified the budget you have to work with. Once you have identified these three things, you are closer to having a successful efficiency improvement launch.

## PLANNING A CRUISE (Create Savings)

## SCENARIO:

Your significant other has unanimously decided the two of you "want" to take an ocean cruise for your tenth anniversary in two years. Since you have learned over the years to pick your battles wisely you have concluded that this is going to happen. With this in mind, you approve the initial investigation and launch the feasibility study.

You have put together a series of steps designed to assist you in reaching your goal of the cruise. What you need is discipline and the ability to judge yourself in order to accomplish these tasks.

While performing a quick search on trying to plan the cruise, you gather enough information to estimate a reasonable cost amount that you will need to take the cruise.   The cruise will be for two people and you have made sure to budget for everything.

The cost breakdown is as follows: The average cost for two tickets on a cruise to your destination is $2800. The cost of two-way airfare to the sea port is $2400 for two people. The total amount of spending money needed will be $600. This trip is estimated to cost around $5800 for two persons.

Some of the remaining scenarios are designed to assist you with your plan to take a cruise in two years. Others are simply efficiency measures that your keen eye came across while reading this book.

## Controlling Expenses

With the plans for taking an Ocean Cruise in two years being inevitable, you begin to focus your energy on ways to make it happen. In order for this to be accomplished, you are going to look for better ways of controlling your expenses.

In this section, we are going to look at the process of controlling money. Instead of talking about spending money, we will focus on investing money in you. Both spending and investing requires money leaving your wallet. However, unlike spending money, investing money means that you are getting more in returns at a later date.

The first thing you should do to better control money is invest a little money in your future. The following two books have given many people the process they need to control money. They are two of many books classified as recommended reading:

*Rich Dad, Poor Dad by Robert Kiyosaki*
*Total Money Makeover by Dave Ramsey*

While the overall guidelines for financial control go beyond the scope of this book, several topics will be discussed in an effort to familiarize you with the concept of efficiency analysis and process improvement.

The best way to save money is to first realize where it is being spent. You also need to be able to identify which transactions are required and which can be reduced. In order to accomplish this task it is best to use software to keep track of your spending.

Companies of all sizes have been using software to track expenses for the past twenty five years. Financial planners and consultants have been instrumental in the industry growth and popularity of accounting software. Accounting software allows financial gurus to quickly review a client's records without having to sort through mountains of paperwork. Many bank branches employ a technical member of staff who can give advice on financial accounting software.

There are many budgeting, bookkeeping and accounting software titles available on the market. You should look for software that is easy to use, usable with your existing bank accounts and low cost. The reasoning for these three traits is as follows.

By selecting easy to use software, you will prevent yourself from having to consume your time studying how to use it. Time is money. It is sometimes cheaper to outsource work than to spend too much learning how to use a tool. However, it is always better to have direct control over your own expenses as this will allow you to see where improvements can be made.

The ability to identify savings becomes even easier if the software is able to import bank account information. Instead of manually typing in all information, a user can save hours per week if they are able to import bank spreadsheets. Once imported, the spreadsheets can be modified to better identify each transaction. Your local bank would be a wealth of information regarding bank compatible software.

Since we are using software to help control expenses, it would make logical sense to choose one that is budget friendly. Some accounting programs on the market sell for hundreds of dollars. These are the ones you should avoid for personal or small business use even though they may offer great benefits.

The author personally recommends GNUCash. This software program is understandable, powerful and free. Once you begin using it or any other accounting software, it becomes much clearer where you are able to save money.

### Is there a demand/need for the process?

YES. People have been using accounting software to monitor expenses for twenty years.

### Who else is using this process?

Almost all businesses use accounting software to monitor expenses.

### What problems can we expect with this process?

Some accounting software does not allow for integration with bank accounts. Not all software allows for editing fields. This is important for customizing information such as "Fixed Cost"/ "Bills" / "Recreation"

### What are resources required to make the process work?

Accounting software and a computer to run the software on are the only two resources needed for this process to work

### What are the costs associated with producing the process?

The only costs are derived from the purchase of the software and a computer if one does not exist. There could also be a cost associated with time required to train on software, analyze the company's information, and input the data into the software.

### Which costs are fixed and which are variable?

Computer and software are one time fixed cost. Training, analysis and inputting data are variable costs.

### How much can we expect to save/gain by implementing this?

You will be able to see where money is being spent and determine which costs are necessities and which costs may be safely eliminated. You will have better control of finances.

# Email Control (Workflow Efficiency)

## SCENARIO:

You have many good ideas on efficiency improvements to make around the house. Unfortunately, as luck would have it, you are too busy working and are unable to focus your attention during the weekend. Your role as supervisor requires you to answer your emails at all hours of the day including when you are at home. Whenever your inbox chimes, you drop everything and come running to tend to your electronic master, even if the email turns out to be spam. In order to give yourself some free time and sanity, you must take action. You want to find a way to reclaim some of your personal time. In order to do this, you must find a way to control distractions.

One method to reclaim your time is to forward important emails to a "VIP" or "immediate response needed" account while leaving normal emails to be reviewed at your convenience. There have been many people who needed the security of following important emails while filtering out less important ones.

This method is used by the author as well as many corporate C-level personnel. It is also popular with university professors. It provides a means of keeping them informed of important topics while not interfering with their day-to-day activities.

You will need a mobile device, a computer for maintenance, and second email account on your mobile device to serve as you filter account. In many cases, these accounts are free of charge by your internet service provider or network administrator.

This method is not without its risks. If an email address is not on your filter list, the email will not be forwarded and can result in a loss of business. This problem can be remedied by requiring the email subject line to begin with a code and set a filter to forward coded messages to your second account.

However, this may lead to a second problem. If the code is not included in the subject line, again the email will not be forwarded. Even though this second problem has no absolute resolution, a safety net can be put into place.

One safety net would require another person to monitor your response time for emails. If you do not respond to an emergency email within 30 minutes, they would contact you via text message or phone call. This will give you enough time to generate a quick response to the email once you see it, but will generate a phone call or text message if you have not replied to it.

As a means of reinforcing this strategy, you should have a standard email reply set up for acknowledgement that message has been received. A simple statement such as "Currently out of the office but I will respond to your email shortly" will give others a clear indication that you have received the email and explain your delayed response. This also gives you time to respond to problem or delegate its resolution.

As we look through the previous information, we find the answers to those important questions regarding feasibility:

### Is there a demand/need for the process?

There have been many people who needed the security of following important emails while filtering out less important ones.

### Who else is using this process?

This method is used by the author as well as many corporate C-level personnel. This method is also very popular with university professors.

### What problems can we expect by switching to this process?

Some important emails will not be forwarded to your second account if the email does not comply with your filter rules. This problem can be overcome but requires training on the part of the sender and an up-to-date email roster. However, the solution is not fool-proof.

### What are the resources required to make the process work?

All you really need is a mobile device, a computer for maintenance and second email account on your mobile device.

### What are the costs associated with producing the process?

If you do not have them, you will need to purchase a mobile device, and a computer for maintenance of your email accounts.

**Which costs are fixed and which are variable?**

The mobile device and the computer for maintenance are both fixed equipment costs. These pieces of equipment are usually deemed routine business costs.

The only variable costs will be those who are incurred for data charges of your mobile device. In many situations, these costs are already an incurred cost of business. If only VIP messages are being transmitted to your mobile device, this can actually reduce the amount of data charges you incur from your device provider.

**How much can we expect to save/gain by implementing this?**

The primary benefit to this is more productive work time with less interruptions. There may also be a decrease in your mobile device carrier, as mentioned earlier with data charges applying only if VIP messages are forwarded to your mobile device.

## Smart Purchasing (Purchasing Control)

### SCENARIO:

Now that you are no longer being annoyed with useless emails, you have more free time. Realizing that your busy schedule has turned your back yard into a sub-tropical rainforest, you decide to go to a local mega-mart store to pick up a few needed lawn maintenance supplies. One hundred thirty seven aisles of super savings greet you as you enter the shrine of the all mighty dollar. The vivid displays and seductive words allure you to generously donate just a few more dollars upon the altar of the bar code scanner.

These temptations go unheard to you, for you are a businessman and immune to such slickly presented temptations. You are here for a few items to tame the wilderness you once coveted as a backyard. All you need is just some lawn bags, a rake, and a weed trimmer. You refuse to leave the store with anything more than these items.

As you move yourself through the twisted maze of lower price signs you finally reach the lawn care area. You have selected the lawn bags and are looking at the trimmers when something catches your eye. "A trimmer on wheels; how silly is that", you think to yourself. Actually, it isn't silly at all! This thing can take down small trees and brush.

You begin to realize that you have not thought about the sprouts of oak trees peeking through the ground. Also, this trimmer has a clipping catcher and bagging system. You will not need the rake or lawn bags if you buy this thing. You receive a lot with this one purchase, albeit $300 more expensive. But this thing has wheels, an easy start engine and safety guard. Anyone will be able to use this amazing marvel of the modern world. Without a moment's hesitation you make your way to the altar and consecrate it with a sacrifice of dead presidents.

You begin to think how this new gadget will change your life as you make your way home. Everyone will be so happy that you purchased something that the whole family can use. You can't wait to see the look on your family member's faces. Nor can you wait to hear their opinion of your savvy buying ability. Upon arrival, you remove the item from the car and summon your family to the garage. Once your family has assembled to view your purchase, you utter those famous last words: "What do you guys think about this?"

At no point in time did you feel that this purchase was going to generate such negative feedback. There was no way for you to know that no one else gave a flying flip about working in the backyard. Nor did you realize that your perception of value differed from those of your family.

Even though you have decided to be more responsible on purchasing decisions, you realize you will still have to make purchases on a regular basis. In order to do this, you must set purchasing controls to prevent you from diving into your savings. How can this can be done? After all, purchasing controls for a business will not work at home; or will they?

At first glance, it may seem there is a large difference between creating purchasing controls for business and home budgets. In reality, purchasing controls are identical between the two entities. The only difference between the two types of purchasing controls is the number of people involved. A large corporation may have hundreds of people who must approve purchases. A household or sole proprietorship may only have one person who approves a purchase. Here lies the problem within the process.

Why do major corporations require so many people to approve a purchases? Is this really efficient for them to have so many? It is true that a major corporation could easily have a single person controlling all purchases? The short answer to both questions is yes. While the corporate practice seems to be a bureaucratic waste of money, this practice has many advantages.

Let us face reality of the situation. A company is only going to staff people to control purchases if the salary of the controller is offset by the amount of money they save. In many cases, a controller's salary will only be a small fraction of the amount of expenses a company saves.

All of these corporate controllers are trained to control a certain type of purchase. They are usually experts in a certain sector of business. They are also aware of the legal implications of a contract and they understand what a supplier can truly deliver at a certain price. This leads to the apparent disadvantage a small business has since they cannot usually afford this level of staffing.

This all sounds wonderful for a large corporation, but what if you run a small company where you make all purchasing decisions? The answer to this question is simple. A small company does not need to primarily focus on purchase controls. A self-managed company needs to first focus on self-control. Self-control for small business purchases requires several small, yet effective, steps.

The first step is to never buy something the first time you see it. When you buy a product the first time you see it, you are actually buying a marketing illusion, not a product. There are millions of people throughout the world who gets paid six-figure salaries to tell stores how you think. Their entire job is to find ways separate you from as much of your money as they can.

Here is a question for you. Have you ever wondered why milk and eggs are always farthest from the entrance of a store? So you must cross aisle after aisle to reach them. As you are crossing them you may spot other items you want but do not need to purchase. Simple, yet very, very effective and efficient.

The second step is to document purchasing strengths for yourself and others around you. Purchasing strength is referring to what areas of information you or others have in-depth knowledge about. A person can be considered an expert if they can stand up at a moment's notice and deliver a fifteen to twenty minute speech about a specific area or topic. If someone cannot do this, they should not be on the list in a specific area. Granted, you may not want to listen to a fifteen minute lecture from Bob on the pros of the ball point versus gel pens. However, if he knows the subject, chances are he will not waste the company's money on pens that fail after two uses.

The third step is to search for advice from an expert for any other topic that appears on the list prior to making any purchase. The experts serve as consultants for their industry. These are the people who require compensation for their advice. Although this may seem an inconvenience, they can save you a lot of money.

### Is there a demand/need for the process?

Yes. Purchase control is considered a necessity for many companies in the world today.

### Who else is using this process?

This process is being used by most companies and by families who are on fixed incomes.

### What problems can we expect by switching to this process?

It is hard to get out of the "buy it if you want it" mentality. During this transition a great deal of self-control will need to be implemented.

### What are the resources required to make the process work?

No resources are required for this process. However, a computer will need to be utilized to research competitive products and compare prices from other venues.

### What are the costs associated with producing the process?

The only associated costs will be that of compensation requirements if someone else conducts the research for you.

### Which costs are fixed and which are variable?

If a computer is needed, it will be a fixed cost. If compensation for a researcher is needed, this will be variable.

### How much can we expect to save/gain by implementing this?

Savings will be measured on a "lack of spending" or on "amount of savings from purchases". The overall savings will be dependent on the amount the process is used.

## Excessive Utility Bills: (Efficiency Measures)

### SCENARIO:

While analyzing your spending, you come across a major financial drain. You notice that you have expensive electric bills. Even though electricity is a requirement for modern lifestyles, you are beginning to wonder if you are paying more than your fair share.

Since you do not work in the energy efficiency industry, you realize that you may be overreacting. With this in mind, you feel that you should conduct your own initial investigation to better be able to determine if you are paying too much or if your costs are in-line with other homeowners in your area.

Since the initial investigation needs to be as accurate as possible, you start looking for ways to establish a baseline. You decide that since you need a baseline, you should talk to neighbors who live in your immediate area since electric costs can vary by location. You also determine that you should look for neighborhood homes of similar size and are of similar age. This should be an easy task since as coincidence would have it, you live in a subdivision where houses were built from the same floor plans, by the same builder, and during the same year.

Over the next few weeks, you meet with a few of your neighbors about their energy usage. While comparing these bills with those of your neighbors, you find that your bills are approximately 30% higher. This does not make sense to you as all of these houses are virtually identical. However, even though these houses are identical, there may be factors causing the differences in utility fees.

Following up on a hunch, you research the energy efficiency improvements found in the HOME PROJECTS section of this book. Armed with this information, you speak to your neighbors again and ask if any of them have used these methods of energy efficiency. To your surprise, they have all found similar advice and implemented it.

You soon determine that you have been looking for the wrong problem. Instead of looking to see if your home was built substandard, you should have been looking to see what others have done to improve their energy efficiency. Now that you realize this new information, you take the time to ask the neighbors what they felt contributed the most to their energy efficiency saving.

The first solution the neighbors all agreed upon was ensuring that your house's heating/cooling system was completely insulated. Your neighbors informed you that thirty percent of their energy waste was attributed to poorly insulated HVAC systems. In many cases, your neighbors found that the ductwork in the basement was sealed enough to pass building inspection but was of minimal quality. Your neighbors paid high initial cost to solve this problem but are reaping rewards after three years.

The second solution that your neighbors recommended was to change all of your incandescent lighting to newer high efficiency LED lighting. These newer generation of light produce as much light as standard bulbs at a fraction of the electric costs. These lights have a higher initial purchase price but can begin to produce savings within a year.

The third recommendation you receive from your neighbors is to use smart electric power strips. These power strips turn off the entire strip if the primary device is powered down. Since plugged in electronic devices always draw electricity, this leads to tremendous savings. This is a useful feature if you have a four bedroom house with a television and peripheral devices in each room. If your TV is the master device and you turn it off, the power strip will also kill power to your DVD player, sound system, and streaming media devices. These units can be purchased for under $50 each. The more units needed will increase initial cost but will usually pay for themselves in one year.

### Is there a demand/need for the process?

Yes. Energy efficiency has become a key cornerstone of today's society.

### Who else is using this process?

Most of your neighbors and many companies are using this process.

### What problems can we expect by switching to this process?

There are no true problems but this is an investment, thus there are higher initial costs.

### What are the resources required to make the process work?

The HVAC requires ductwork.

The lighting solution requires LED bulbs.

The electric control requires specialty power strips.

### What are the costs associated with producing the process?

The HVAC costs can be a few hundred dollars.

The LED lights can be a hundred dollars, depending on number of lights.

The power strips can be a few hundred dollars. Each unit can be purchased for under $50.

**Which costs are fixed and which are variable?**

All costs associated will be fixed costs since you will only have to purchase once.

**How much can we expect to save by implementing this?**

Absolute savings will be determined by the amount of upgrades you do to your home.

RESULTS: If all upgrades are performed, they are expected to collectively pay for themselves within the first two years at current utility usage.

# Reducing Debt

## SCENARIO:

In the world of personal and business finance there is only one primary rule you ever need to know: the more available credit you have access to, you will be positioned better. The key word here is "available". It is not uncommon to see people with a large amount of credit and just as much debt. People and companies both realize the crippling effects high debt has on them. Compound interest are two of the most damning words in finance, unless you are a bank. Then it's okay.

If you are not too sure what compounding interest is, here is an example. Have you ever noticed that your credit card bills do not seem to be reducing no matter what you money pay on them? Voila! The hidden demonic source which siphons away all of the money you use to pay bills is the best way to view compounding interest.

In many circumstances, people do not realize the problem is bad until it is almost completely out of control. This leads to people scrambling to find any way they can to bring their debt back under control. If that isn't bad enough, people trying to reduce debt lose hundreds of dollars each year to debt consolidation companies who teach them to follow the advice presented here.

The good news is that this is not a hard problem to correct, although it takes discipline. The solution requires you to reduce or eliminate "fun" money reserves and redirect it to reducing your debts. While this may seem like a harsh penalty, anyone who is financially educated and truly concerned about debt reduction uses this method. In addition, many banks and credit unions will deliver this advice to their customers as a means of keeping more money in the bank. Lucky for consumers, banks don't like others taking money they feel is rightfully their money.

There are only two primary steps to this process. The first step is to create a realistic budget. A budget can be created by the end user or you can seek professional help to create it. Having someone else to create your budget may seem like a waste of money but it is well worth the expense.

The second step is what causes problems with most people: Stick to the budget you created. The creation of a budget does no good if you do not follow it. This step requires discipline and self-control. This is the most important part of any debt reduction.

### Is there a demand/need for the process?

Yes. People and companies both realize the crippling effects high debt has on them. People trying to reduce debt lose hundreds of dollars each year to debt consolidation companies who teach them to follow the advice presented here.

### Who else is using this process?

Anyone who is financially educated and truly concerned about debt reduction uses this method. Many banks and credit unions will deliver this advice to their customers as a means of keeping more money in the bank.

### What problems can we expect with this process?

You will experience initially high payouts and will have less "fun" money. Entertainment activities will be reduced while debt reduction is underway.

### What are the resources required for this process?

You will need a realistic and reasonable budget prepared by a financial planner, a banking advisor, or yourself. You will need will-power and some financial savings to properly do this.

### What are the costs associated with producing the process?

You will need savings or disposable income in order to reduce debt efficiently.

### Which costs are fixed and which are variable?

All costs for this will be variable unless you choose to use a financial planner to create your initial budget.

### How much can we expect to save by implementing this?

As an end result you can reduce your financial loss by the amount of compounding interest you would have paid before launching this debt reduction campaign.

# Cooking (Queueing Theory)

## SCENARIO:

The cold days of winter are now creeping into non-existence. Your routine of finding a sweater has been replaced with finding a nice shirt. Even though the days of donning swimwear is getting near, you feel that something is missing. As fate would have it, your toes are those missing things.

Albeit a bit depressing, you are not really surprised by your findings. Your heavy work schedule has forced you to choose eating at fast food restaurants instead of eating healthier meals. It hasn't really been much of a choice. After all, you only have so many minutes to cook and eat before you are out the door on another endeavor.

In the fast paced lifestyle of today's family it is not unheard of for **people to eat two or three meals a day in restaurants**. This practice leads to unhealthy eating conditions as well as places a huge strain on your financial resources. In many cases, people blame this habit mostly on time constraints instead of their own self-discipline. No matter the reason for constantly eating out, you have an easy way of fixing it.

Throughout the culinary world there is a marvelous device known as a slow cooker. This item allows you to throw in a large chunk of meat, place it on the low setting and it is thoroughly cooked in eight to ten hours. This unit was widely used during the 1970s and 1980s when in the United States women began working outside of the home while still being responsible for household chores.

The slow cooker has come a long way since it was first introduced in 1970 but it functions the same way. As a matter of fact, the Rival slogan for the Crock Pot was "cooks all day while the cook's away". Even though its sales declined with the introduction of the microwave, it is still a powerful asset to have in the kitchen. As interesting as it may be, we will now conclude the historical account of the slow cooker.

In order to be able to keep a good healthy diet going throughout the work week, people must begin to rely on weekends or off-days for cooking multiple meals. The method of cooking meals for a whole week is not new. It has been used for many years, although most modern families have forgotten about the practice. If you were born before the 1970s you probably witnessed this phenomena firsthand.

The concept is to cook bulky meat items on the weekends and store most of it for later consumption. For instance, instead of cooking a pound of chicken parts on Saturday, you will slow cook a whole four or five pound chicken with vegetables. You will consume one to two pounds and store the rest in storage containers, each containing one and a half pounds of meat. On Sunday, you will repeat this process using Lamb, Beef or Pork. Once again, you will consume one to two pounds and reserve the rest in containers. You will also reserve the remaining vegetables.

Even though it cooks quickly, you might want to consider precooking some pasta and storing them in airtight storage bags. This will give you a quick meal option in the event that things change and your limited time becomes even more limited. Chicken, lamb, beef and pork can all be mixed with pasta and a few other ingredients to make a quick meal. Rice works even better but is harder to store and reheat.

Once the weekend is over and you return to your busy lifestyle, you have enough precooked meat items for the week. At this stage, meals can be constructed in a matter of minutes. Most pastas cook in 5 to 12 minutes depending on variety and rice cooks in about 20 minutes with little work on your part. Alternatively, you can find your favorite slow cooker recipe book and cook meals daily using the precooked meats. It is usually best to have a smaller slow cooker on hand for daily meal cooking.

As an added benefit to this healthier approach to cooking, you will save a lot of money on the process. The same $20 it takes to purchase three sub-par meals at a local fast-food restaurant, can be used to purchase a 4-5 pound chicken and five pound pork roast. These two items can provide a week's worth of meat for meals.

There are some concerns from people as they may not get home from work in time to keep the slow cooker from overcooking their meals. Luckily, we have technology to take care of that problem. If you set a programmable electric timer control, the same kind used for Christmas lights, you can cut off the electricity after eight hours. The ceramic vessel of the slow cooker will keep the item at safe temperature for several more hours. It will not continue cooking but it won't immediately start cooling either. This really is a marvelous device.

Let there be no mistake: the process of cooking your meats early can be done with a conventional stove or oven. The largest drawback is that a stove requires more supervision and will need to be monitored frequently as the cooking process nears completion. Also, you should not leave the stove cooking without someone monitoring. This is where the slow cooker gains its greatest advantage.

### Is there a demand/need for the process?

Yes. The complexity of day to day life requires everyone to think ahead about how they will eat their meals

### Who else is using this process?

If you need to find people who use tricks for cooking meals, look no further than your local college or university. Students become very resourceful when it comes to cooking meals while balancing class schedule and study time.

### What problems can we expect by switching to this process?

You will need to learn the capabilities of the slow cooker and how to properly use it. There may also be times when you will not be able to be home right when the cooking process should end. This problem can be overcome using electronic timing circuit.

### What are the resources required to make the process work?

The author recommends purchasing one large and one small slow cookers. It is also recommended that you purchase one or two electronic timing circuits that can be programmed for 24 hour usage.

### What are the costs associated with producing the process?

Both slow cookers will cost about $65 total, the electronic timer will cost about $15.

**Which costs are fixed and which are variable?**

The costs of slow cookers are fixed, the cost of electric usage will be variable.

**How much can we expect to save by implementing this?**

There is no way to determine the amount of actual savings. However, if you are accustomed to eating 2-3 meals a day from a fast-food restaurant, your savings will be major. The primary savings will be delivered in the form of time savings.

Not enough Toilet Paper (Inventory Control)

SCENARIO:

It has been one of the most beautiful non-working days that you can remember. The warm sun has caressed you with its seemingly never-ending rays of wholesome vitamin D. It got to be a bit warm in the park at times, but this was nothing that a few tall glasses of tea could not remedy. Even though it seems too soon, the sun is starting to clock-out for the day and head for home. With a sense of dread, you decide to do the same. It really has been a beautiful day at the park.

While saying goodbye to the park, you begin your long commute to the other side of the city. The serenity and openness of the park is soon replaced by the anxiety and congestion of the roadways. The stop and go, bumper-to-bumper traffic is leaving the impression of waves crashing against a tiny ship in a large ocean. Speaking of oceans, with every stop you are really starting to regret that last large tea. Oh my, this trip seems to be getting longer.

You are only one interstate off-ramp away from exiting to the serenity of your neighborhood, but your mind remains paranoid about what all could go wrong to cause a delay. With every press of the brake pedal, you visualize violent ocean waves being generated from demons within a hurricane. This visualization continues until you press the brake in your car port.

You decide to leave your items in your car as you enter the house to take care of more pressing matters and hastily make your way to the bathroom whose door has opened as if it was Heaven's gate. You made it!

It is at this point you look over and realize that someone in your home forgot to put on a fresh roll of toilet paper.

Whether business or personal, nothing is more devastating than running out of a resource. It is what we emphatically call a showstopper. Regardless of whether you choose to admit this or not, everyone has experienced this type of shortage. If you're lucky, you discover it at a noncritical time.

As you contemplate your current predicament your mind begins to wonder how you can avoid this situation in the future. This is where the formulation of an inventory control process officially begins. Many questions are asked at this point in time. How did you get in the situation? What could you have done to prevent this supply chain fiasco? What is the best way to keep this from happening in the future?

Once the near crisis has been dealt with, you decide to prevent its recurrence by establishing inventory controls. However, before you can make such controls, you need to understand what controls are available to you. The best way to understand what controls are available is to speak to others who already have controls in place.

To accomplish this, you should talk to a person who owns a business with a high number of on-site customers, which is not a grocery store. The reason you exclude grocery stores is they can supplement their private inventory with their sales inventory. This is considered to be a cheating move for this scenario.

A restaurant would be an ideal place to begin your investigation. Restaurants have a high number of on-site customers. We are going to make the assumption that restaurants are unlikely to be selling toilet paper to customers. (This assumption was valid at the time this book was being written.) We are going to make the further assumption that you have access to a friend you feel comfortable speaking with on such matters and who owns a restaurant. This is a difficult subject; just roll with it please.

If we were to investigate how restaurant utilizes inventory controls for non-mission items such as toilet paper, we see they primarily use it reorder point method. The reorder point is determined by the availability of free space for non-mission inventory and the delivery method of non-mission inventory.

For example, let us suppose a restaurant receives paper product deliveries once every two weeks. In this instance, the manager will ensure the restaurant has at least two weeks supply of paper products such as drinking cups, napkins, and toilet paper. In many cases the manager will try to keep an additional two weeks of supplies on hand to compensate for a delayed or incomplete delivery.

Out of all the scenarios, inventory control is the hardest to emulate inside of the home. The reason it is so difficult to emulate is because very few supplies are critical inside of the home. If you run out of milk for cereal, you can eat toast for breakfast. If you run out of soft drinks, you can drink water. If you run out of dishwashing liquid, the dishes will just be dirty for one more day. Indeed, this is a difficult problem to emulate because running out of supplies at home is much less tragic.

Inventory controls are designed to keep businesses from running out of critical supplies at a critical moment. There are certain supplies that would cripple a business if it were to not have them on hand. Therefore, inventory control processes are a primary component of most businesses large or small.

In order for you to create a good example of inventory control inside the home you are forced to go to the extreme. You're going to have to face a major crisis! You're going to have to go to a code red scenario. That is exactly what was done!

### Is there a demand/need for the process?

Yes. There are certain supplies that would cripple a business if it were to not have them on hand.

### Who else is using this process?

Inventory control processes are a primary component of most businesses large or small. A restaurant would be an ideal place to begin your investigation.

### What problems can we expect by switching to this process?

You will need space for an additional two weeks of supplies on hand to compensate for a delayed or incomplete delivery.

### What are the resources required to make the process work?

You will need available free space for non-mission inventory and the delivery method.

### What are the costs associated with producing the process?

You may need to purchase additional shelves to accommodate an increase in storage for inventory. You will also need to purchase the additional inventory.

**Which costs are fixed and which are variable?**

Whatever shelving you need to purchase to accommodate an increase in supplies will be your fixed costs. The inventory itself will be the variable costs.

**How much can we expect to save by implementing this?**

In this circumstance, the savings are more of a convenience. The primary savings here is time. The true financial savings would only equal a few dollars per month, but efficiency should never be measured by money. (See Myths About Efficiency section)

OK, You can call the contractor now.

## SECTION A. – SAVE MONEY ON UTILITIES

*HEATING:*

About 40 percent of your total home energy budget goes for heating. Improving efficiency in this area will go a long way to saving a lot of money. Below are some tips that can reduce your heating bills.

Use a programmable thermostat and program (or dial down) it to 67 degrees when you are home and 55 degrees when you are away. Most people have the same every day routine. If you teach your routine to your programmable thermostat, you can save huge amounts of money. Furthermore, it never forgets to turn down the heat.

When you go to bed, turn your thermostat to 55 degrees. This can save 15% on your nightly heating bill. More than 90% of your house is unused while you are sleeping.

In case you are concerned about being cold at night, using an electric blanket can take the chill out of cold nights and uses 1/3 to 1/2 of the total energy required for a space heater. Heat only what you need. Using an extra blanket will allow you to lower the temperature in your home while you are sleeping.

Have your heating system tuned and inspected by a service professional before each heating season. Clean or replace the furnace filter often. If you decide to replace your furnace, look for one that's at least 90 percent efficient. Use supplemental heating equipment for hard-to-heat areas.

Close your attic, basement, garage and exterior doors to prevent cold drafts and keep in heat. Installing a curtain rod over exterior doors will allow you to use thermal curtains to catch cold air that gets past weather-stripping. Do not block heat registers or air return ducts.

*COOLING:*

### For All types of Cooling

1. Do not cool unused areas. Close registers and doors to rooms not required to be cooled.
2. Set air conditioning thermostat to 78 degrees when you are home.
3. Make sure that the filter is cleaned regularly.
4. Ceiling fans cool fast and require 1/4 the energy to operate.
5. Attic fans can get rid of excess heat trapped in the attic.

### For Central Units

1. If you have a central unit make sure that it is the right size to cool the area.
2. Remove leaves and debris away from the outside unit.

### For Window Units

1. Install air conditioners in the shade. Direct sunlight causes it to use more energy.
2. Close heating vents to prevent air from escaping into them.

1. Heating water accounts for the third largest cost associated with energy use. It accounts for approximately 15%.

2. Take a shower instead of a bath. This saves on water usage and the energy needed for water heating. Double savings.

3. Install a flow restrictor or aerator. Once again, this saves on water usage and the energy needed for water heating. Another Double savings.

4. When you are away for a few days, set your hot water heater thermostat to the Vacation setting or Low setting.

5. Set your hot water heater thermostat to 120 degrees. This is sometimes represented as medium-low setting on some water heaters. The entire concept of heated water is more for comfort not for the bathing process itself.

6. Turn off hot water when not in use. An inch or two of hot water in a bathroom sink is sufficient for washing or shaving. Rinsing can be done with cool water.

7. Fix dripping faucets or leaking pipes. A small cold water leak may cost $30 to $40 extra per month. A small hot water leak can cost $60 to $80 extra. Plumbing sealant only costs $3 - $5.

8. Install an insulating blanket around a hot water heater hold in heat. This reduces the energy needed to heat up water.

9. Drain your hot water heater at least once per year.

## DISH WASHER

Dish Washers increase both water usage and heating energy. Here are some tips.

1. If you have time, wash dishes in a sink or tub. You will save on both water usage and heating energy.
2. Set dishwasher to low setting.
3. Wash only full loads.
4. Use the shortest run cycle.
5. Use the no-heat drying setting.
6. Clean the drain every week or two.
7. Pre-soak pots and pans. Hand washing will be better for them anyways.

1. Only Wash full loads. The same amount of electricity is used regardless of load size.

2. Properly measure detergents. Less is better than more.

3. Set the water level to match the load size.

4. Use cold water, when able, coupled with cold water detergents.

5. Wash bras (or other delicates) in the sink. Saves water, energy and cost of replacing the garment.

6. Do not over dry clothes. Damp dry and hang them up.

7. Clean the lint trap after each use.

8. Hang clothing out on sunny days.

9. For multiple wash loads. Fill the dryer as soon as it has stopped. A pre-warmed dryer uses less energy.

A device that operates closest to its operating temperature will have less malfunctions. In order to get the most efficient use of your refrigerator, you need to set its thermostat to 38 - 42 degrees Fahrenheit. To get the most efficient use of your freezer, you should set its thermostat to 0 degrees - 5 degrees Fahrenheit. These are the optimal operating temperatures for these devices. The optimal temperatures for refrigerators/freezers are established by the capability of the condenser coils.

Speaking of the condenser coils, it is recommended by manufacturers to clean refrigerator/freezer condenser coils at least twice a year. Even though no one has stated the best two times of year to clean condenser coils, logic reminds us that dust, pollen and airborne pollutant count is highest during the Spring and Fall of each year. Dust, pollen and airborne pollutant are the elements which can restrict airflow and prevent the condenser coils from operating normally.

Another factor that creates a lack of airflow on the condenser coils is proximity to other immobile structures. Do not enclose refrigerators and freezers where the condenser coils cannot extract heat from the units. By pulling the units away from walls, you can create an airflow path for the condenser coils.

A third factor that affects the cooling ability is some people forget to cool down their cooked food before they store it in the refrigerator or freezer. This increases the internal temperature and forces the unit to work harder. Allow hot food to cool for about an hour before storing.

Laws of thermodynamics states that the temperature maintenance is relative to the amount of mass in an area. In plain English this means more items (mass) you keep inside of your refrigerator/freezer the more constant the temperature will be. However, Even though it is best to keep your refrigerator and freezer full, you should not keep them packed as this will affect air flow.

Another trick to maintain constant temperature is to place water filled containers in empty spaces of your refrigerator & freezer. The water will hold its temperature longer during blackouts and will keep the units closer to their operating temperatures. This also serves as additional protection in the event of a power outage.

The last bit of advice for refrigerators and freezers is to keep the temperature as constant as possible. If you minimize the number of times the doors are opened and the duration they are opened you will save a great deal of money. You should also check door seals and replace them if they allow cold air to leak out.

Plumbing, while not considered a major contributor to utility waste is the least efficient part of most homes. Water is used throughout the day but only a fraction of the water is actually used. Most of the water returns to the utility board. This is like taking a single bite from a hamburger and throwing the rest away. Even though this is considered normal everyday accepted practice, up until 100 years ago people would have considered this practice wasteful and absolute madness.

Even though we cannot control the wasteful social practice that our culture tells us is normal, we can control our own wastefulness. Water usage can be made more efficient if you know a few tricks. The long term end results will be a dramatically reduced water bill.

## Water and Sewer Usage Fees

Most water boards that also control sewer systems use the amount of water you use to determine the sewer liability (fees) that you owe. Therefore, if you purchase or build a water recycling/purification system, you can actually recycle water from your sink, shower, or bathtub for reuse in a non-food water system such as a toilet, shower, bathtub, outdoor sprinkler system or car pressure washer. This method of recycling is known as grey water system recycling.

Furthermore, if you add a water storage tank, you will actually be able to control when and where the water is used. Many of the storage tanks that hold under 300 gallons can be placed on the back of a pickup or small trailer. You can find 275 gallon plastic water storage container in many stores for under $200.

## Use You Own Water

I have already showed you how you can recycle your own water in order to save on water sewer fees. The next step is to show you how to reduce them even further with a little help from Mother Nature.

When water plumbing/irrigation was first used, long before water utilities services, people relied on three ways to collect water. Once collected, the water would hopefully be purified either through filtration or boiling.

The first method is to use water from a river or stream. This method required people to divert, carry or pump water from a river or stream to the point of use. This method has been around for tens of thousands of years in farming areas, but was greatly refined for home use with the development of the Roman Aqueducts & Cisterns. Most water utilities throughout the world still use this method to collect water for purification.

The second method was to draw/pump water from a well. This method required people to pipe or use buckets to carry water to the point of use. Wells were commonly used by urban people throughout the United States until the mid-1900s. There are many wells still used today in farming areas, albeit extremely more modernized.

The third method is to build a rainwater collection system. This method was the most common type found throughout the United States. Most homes in drier regions of the country had a rainwater collection system. Most of the rainwater collection systems were nothing more than a barrel or trough at the corner of a structure that collected rain as it fell from the building.

## SECTION B: COOKING

Cooking is an area that people do not think about when the word efficiency is mentioned.

Day one:  Roast Chicken and Vegetables

1 (4-5  lb.) roasting chicken (whole)

4 cloves garlic, halved

For the Rub:

3 tsp. Kosher salt

1 tsp. smoked paprika

1 tsp. dried thyme

1 tsp. black pepper

½ tsp. garlic powder

½ tsp. onion powder

½ C. turnips, diced (3 small)

1 ¼ C. carrots, scrubbed and cut into 3-inch chunks (6 small)

¾ C. parsnips, scrubbed and cut into 3-inch chunks (2 small)

1 C. Yukon Gold potatoes, peeled and cut into 1-inch cubes (2 small)

**Directions:**
Place all ingredients in the slow cooker on low setting and walk away for 8 hours. When finished, reserve 2-3 lbs of chicken (skin and bones removed) and place in storage containers. You should have two more meals available from containers. Do the same for the leftover vegetables. Place containers in refrigerator or freezer.

Day Two: Chicken Fettuccine

    Kosher salt

    12 ounces fettuccine

    Olive oil, for tossing

    12 ounces precooked chicken

    Freshly ground black pepper

    2 tablespoons unsalted butter

    1 1/2 cups freshly grated Parmigiano-Reggiano cheese

    1 jar Alfredo Sauce

**Directions:**

Bring a large pot of water to a boil, and salt generously. Add the pasta, and boil according to package directions until al dente, tender but still slightly firm. Strain, and toss with a splash of oil.

Meanwhile, dice the chicken into 1/4-inch-thick strips, and lay them on a plate or a sheet of waxed paper. Season with salt and pepper.

Heat a large skillet over medium heat, and add 2 tablespoons of the butter until melted. Transfer the chicken to a medium bowl.

Reduce the heat to medium and add the contents of the Alfredo sauce. Lower the heat to keep the sauce just warm. Whisk the Parmigiano-Reggiano into the sauce. Add the chicken and cooked pasta, and toss well. Season with salt and pepper. Serve hot

Day Three: Chicken Fried Rice

1 Egg

1 tablespoon water

1 tablespoon butter

1 tablespoon vegetable oil

1 onion, chopped

2 cups cooked white rice, cold

2 tablespoons soy sauce

1 teaspoon ground black pepper

1 cup cooked, chopped chicken meat

**Directions:**
In a small bowl, beat egg with water. Melt butter in a wok or large skillet over medium low heat. Add egg and leave flat for 1 to 2 minutes. Remove from skillet and cut into shreds.

Heat oil in same skillet; add onion and sauté until soft. Then add rice, soy sauce, pepper and chicken. Stir fry together for about 5 minutes, then stir in egg. Serve hot.

# BEEF

Day one: Beef Roast and vegetables

3 to 4-pound bottom round beef roast

1/2 to 1 teaspoon salt

1/2 teaspoon fresh ground pepper

2 Tablespoons olive oil

3 garlic cloves, smashed and peeled

16 baby red potatoes

4 large carrots, peeled, sliced in 1-inch pieces

1/2 cup beef broth

**Directions:**

Season beef roast with salt and pepper.

Heat oil in stovetop-safe cookware over medium-high heat. Brown roast well on both sides.

Surround roast with potatoes and carrots. Pour beef broth over everything. Cover and place cookware on slow cooker base. Cook on LOW for 8 hours. Walk away for 8 hours.

Remove roast to serving platter. Using slotted spoon, remove vegetables to serving platter with roast. Cover with foil to keep warm. Reserve 3 pounds of beef for other recipes.

Day Two: Beef Stew

3 tablespoons olive oil

1 tablespoon butter

2 pounds beef stew meat

3 cloves garlic, minced

1 medium onion, diced

4 cups beef broth, more as needed

1 tablespoon Worcestershire sauce

2 to 3 tablespoons tomato paste

1 1/2 teaspoons sugar

1/2 teaspoon paprika

1/2 teaspoon kosher salt

Freshly ground black pepper

2 carrots, roughly sliced

2 parsnips, roughly sliced

1 small turnip, roughly sliced

2 tablespoons all-purpose flour, optional

**Directions:**

Throw all ingredients in the slow cooker on low setting and walk away for 8-10 hours. Come back at end of day, stir and serve the mixture, reserve the rest for tomorrow.

Day Three: Beef Tips and Rice

- 1lb precooked Beef, cut into bite size pieces
- 3 cups Beef Broth
- 1 Tablespoon vegetable oil
- 2 Tablespoons Cornstarch
- Salt and Pepper to taste
- 2-3 cups of cooked Rice

**Directions:**

1. Cut beef into about one inch cubes.
2. Place a medium sized sauce pot on medium-high heat.
3. Add cooking oil.
4. Add beef and beef broth, bring to a rolling boil.
5. Cover, reduce heat to medium
6. In a small bowl, mix Cornstarch with cold water, stir well.
7. Slowly add the cornstarch to the beef and broth, stirring constantly.
8. Simmer another 10 minutes or until gravy has thickened.
9. Spoon rice into a bowl, cover with beef tips, Enjoy.

## Day one: Ham and Vegetables

5 Lbs Ham (cut as needed to fit)

7 Carrots sliced and cut into thirds

10-12 Small Whole Potatoes

1 tsp Fresh Ground Pepper

Water Enough to cover

**Directions:**

Place vegetables then ham in the slow cooker.

Turn slow cooker on "Low" setting.

Find something to do for the next 8 hours.

Upon completion, turn off the slow cooker. Carve away what you need for your meal. Enjoy your hard work.

When finished eating, segment ham into approximately 1 ½ lbs sections and place in storage containers. You should have two more meals available from containers. Do the same for the leftover vegetables. Place containers in refrigerator or freezer.

Day Two: Ham & Cheese Quiche

- 1 package (14.1 ounces) refrigerated pie pastry
- 2 cups diced fully cooked ham
- 2 cups (8 ounces) shredded sharp cheddar cheese
- 4 large eggs
- 2 cups half-and-half cream
- 1/2 teaspoon salt
- 1/4 teaspoon pepper

**Directions:**

Preheat oven to 400°. Prepare pastry shell to recommended instructions.

Divide ham and cheese between shells. In a large bowl, whisk eggs, cream, salt and pepper until blended. Pour into shells. Cover edges loosely with foil. Bake 35-40 minutes or until a knife inserted near the center comes out clean. Let stand 5-10 minutes before cutting. Yield: 2 quiches (6 servings each).

This dish is best prepared the night before and it reheats extremely well.

Day Three: Ham and Bean Soup

Ingredients

- 10 bacon strips, diced
- 1 large onion, chopped
- 1 cup diced carrots
- 3 tablespoons all-purpose flour
- 3 cups milk
- 1-1/2 cups water
- 2-1/2 cups cubed potatoes
- 1 can (15-1/4 ounces) whole kernel corn, drained
- 2 teaspoons chicken bouillon granules
- Pepper to taste
- 3 cups (12 ounces) shredded cheddar cheese
- 1-2 cups cubed fully cooked ham

Take all ingredients and place in the slow cooker on low for 8 hours. Go find something to do for 8 hours.

Day Four: Ham and Cheese Omelet

2 Eggs

2 Tbsp. water

1 tsp. butter

Salt and pepper

1/4 cup shredded favorite cheese blend

1/4 cup finely chopped ham

**Directions:**

BEAT eggs and water in small bowl until blended.

In a 8-inch nonstick omelet pan or skillet warm ham. Remove ham and add butter to pan melting over medium-high heat until hot. Place. POUR IN egg mixture. The mixture should begin to set immediately at edges.

Gently move cooked portions from edges toward the center with inverted turner so that uncooked eggs can reach the hot pan surface.

When top surface of eggs is thickened and no visible liquid egg remains, season with salt and pepper. Place cheese on one side of omelet and top with ham. Fold omelet in half with turner. Use the turner to slide omelet onto plate. SERVE immediately.

A quick, hearty and inexpensive dish that can be served any time of day.

# REFERENCES:

Flowchart Image, <u>NC Department of Environment and Natural Resources</u>, http://quality.enr.state.nc.us/tools/flowchart.htm

Godin, Seth. Tribes: We Need You to Lead Us. Penguin Books Ltd. New York. 2008.

Kiyosaki, Robert T., and Sharon L Lechter. Rich Dad, Poor Dad: What the Rich Teach Their Kids About Money-- That the Poor and Middle Class Do Not! TechPress, 1998.

Miller, Danny. The Icarus paradox: How exceptional companies bring about their own downfall. Business Horizons, Vol. 35, No. 1. (January 1992), pp. 24-35 by

Ramsey, Dave. "Total Money Makeover." Dave Ramsey. The Lampo Group, 2008. Web. 8 May 2016.


Honorable Mentions:

"J.K.Rowling Official Site." J.K.Rowling Official Site - Harry Potter and More. N.p., n.d. Web. 8 May 2016.

Mastic, Debra. The Common Sense Resume: A Practical and Reliable Guide to Resumes Paperback. 2016